THE INVENTION OF ZERO

Chris Greenhalgh won a Gregory Award in 1992. He has published three collections with Bloodaxe: *Stealing the Mona Lisa* (1994), *Of Love, Death and the Sea-Squirt* (2000), and now *The Invention of Zero* (2007). His novel *Coco and Igor*, for which he has written a screenplay, was published by Headline in 2002.

Born in Manchester, he lived for several years in Italy and Athens before returning to the UK to complete a doctoral thesis on postmodern American poetry. He currently teaches at Sevenoaks School in Kent.

CHRIS GREENHALGH

THE
INVENTION
OF
ZERO

BLOODAXE BOOKS

ISBN: 978 1 85224 773 7

First published 2007 by
Bloodaxe Books Ltd,
Highgreen,
Tarset,
Northumberland NE48 1RP.

www.bloodaxebooks.com
For further information about Bloodaxe titles
please visit our website or write to
the above address for a catalogue.

Bloodaxe Books Ltd acknowledges
the financial assistance of
Arts Council England, North East.

Cover design: Neil Astley & Pamela Robertson-Pearce.

Cover printing: J. Thomson Colour Printers Ltd, Glasgow.

Printed in Great Britain by
Bell & Bain Limited, Glasgow, Scotland.

for Ruth, Saul and Ethan

CONTENTS

There is infinitely more nothing in the universe than anything else.

JOHN UPDIKE, *The Poorhouse Fair*

The Invention of Zero

Nature adores a vacuum –
a few bits of light
snagged on nothingness.

We descend into Heathrow.
Arteries of traffic glow
like a dye injected into the blood.

Office windows flash their patterns –
lit and black, like the ones and zeros
of binary code.
The river is a broad gap of darkness.

Back home on the answerphone,
there's a rubbed spot on the surface
of the silence
where voices have been erased.

And like the perfect circle Giotto
drew to win a commission,
there it is through the window –

the moon –
white beyond bleaching,
the end of abstraction;

a perfect blank.

The Undersea World of Jacques Cousteau

While my mother chokes on a fish-bone,
I am shuffled into another room

to watch *The Undersea World of Jacques Cousteau*.
Bubbles rush upwards from

a diver's mouthpiece
as my mother coughs up blood.

Beyond the window,
snowflakes rim the leafless trees.

The deep teems with presences.
My mother's face takes on

a distressing error in form. The ocean
generates a sad music all its own.

Ambulance lights dye the snow blue.
A siren bends the air to zero.

Lines

It is true: every
kink
is merely an
inflection
on a straight
line, like the
thin continuous
wire composing
the main cable
of a suspension
bridge, the plaited
ropes of a swing
unravelling backwards,
a Möbius strip, or
an appleskin un-
peeling in one
ribbonlike piece.
Invisible strings of
attraction draw us
together – my
father's gestures
folded into my own,
my own woven
into my son's and,
who knows, God's
folded into
all of us.
      The
lines extend to
a vanishing point,
where our
two bloods meet
unseen.

The Clock of the Long Now

To encourage people to
slow down,
a group of prominent Americans
has bought a small Nevada mountain
on which they plan to erect
a huge timepiece.

This 'Clock of the Long Now'
will tick once a year,
chime once a century and,
once every 10,000 years,
a cuckoo will come out.

At the Driving Range

(for Chris Fletcher)

Afterwards at the bar,
you tell two women
that you're an optician,
and in a twin impulse they fish
pairs of glasses from their bags.
You know what to do.
Leaning over, you slip off
each pair in turn and
make fussy adjustments
to the bridges and arms –
little tweaks here and there –
before replacing them on
their stunned upturned faces.
The colour of their drinks
turns green under the lights.

But first you address the ball
with a familiar shimmy,
and complete the arc
of a perfect swing.
The clubhead flashes like a wand
in your hands. The ball rises
high from the second storey,
hovers for a moment
above the floodlit grass,
shrinks to a star and
becomes vanishingly small,
swallowed by shadows, lost
amid sandtraps, rabbits,
trembling daisies –
out of sight.

Portraits de Femmes

1

She carried a revolver but no toothbrush.
The Arabs talked of her as a man.
Lionised by the romantic armchair traveller
of the early twentieth century as
'The Amazon of the Sahara',
Isabelle Eberhardt
perished in a flash-flood
at Ain Sefra, Morocco.

Her body, dressed as an Arab cavalryman,
was discovered on the first floor
of a small clay house. Apparently
she had not tried to escape.
Whether she died by accident or design is not known,
but her diaries point to
a Muslim admiration for those who
'folded their arms' in the face of death.

2

Poise is everything
as Laforgue understood –
his Salomé
            at the moment of
stretching
            losing her
balance as she
jettisoned the head
of Iokanaan from
a sheer promontory
into the sea.

3 *Cora Pearl*

Known to her clients
as *l'agenouillée* –
'the kneeling one'

the Second Empire starlet
enlivened dinner parties
by serving herself naked for dessert

surrounded by
meringues
and dusted with sugar

on a silver platter
she'd borrowed from
the Prince d'Orléans –

one unpeeled grape set
like an emerald
in her navel.

4

Re – the love affairs of the Jewess Rachel,
                              the celebrated actress,
the first time she lost her virtue:
the Prince of Joinville,
            son of Louis Philippe (Admiral of France)
had just brought home Napoleon's ashes...

At a gala night at the Comédie Française
given in his honour,
he saw Rachel and at once sent a message
to her box with the words,

Où? Quand? Combien?
to which she replied,
Ce soir, chez moi, pour rien!
And the two had a priceless time.

Picture This

A dandelion left on
sensitised paper.
Daylight does the rest.

Stars hardened from gas
ponderously clotted –
holes in the blackness congealed.

Take Louis Daguerre's shot
of a boulevard:
the exposure so slow

the people fail to show
so that only
a man stopping

to bend low
and have his shoes shined
leaks through.

Or the split-second
it takes for Hiroshima
to be solarised –

the flash so fierce
it makes shadows
of the inhabitants,

light penetrating a laboratory
to develop
the photographs of ghosts.

It's darker than it ought to be.
It's later than we think.
I set the lens to infinity and click.

Thataway

(after Holan)

pushing back her hair,
playing with her ring,
laughing ostentatiously, flirting.

The fountain gushed smeary colours.
Pinkish hibiscus lights threw
petals at our feet.
I realised later

when I'd asked her
the way to the nearest bar,
she'd sent me the wrong way
deliberately.

Arnold Schoenberg

He would mark the numbers of his bars
12, 12A, then 14.
He elided the second 'a'
from Moses und Aron
so that the letters would not
add up to thirteen.

He feared he would die
in a year of his life
that was a multiple of *that* number.

'It's not a superstition,' he said,
'it's a belief!'

39, 52 and 65 came and went,
and he breathed a sigh of relief.
He knew he was safe until 78.

But on Friday, July 13, 1951
at quarter to midnight,
at the age of just 76,
death came with its atonal knock,
whispering into his ear
how the two digits 7 and 6
together make thirteen.

Constantin Cavafy

Aged twenty-nine, he was appointed

the next twenty years.

His poems, meanwhile, gathered
the way scratches on aluminium
organise themselves in circles
around a light.

Shortly before succumbing to
cancer of the larynx,
he received communion
in the Orthodox Church.

His mouth opened
round as his spectacles.
No words came –
just a tiny glottal sob.

His last act: to draw
a circle
on a blank piece of paper
and in the middle
a full stop.

I Confess

(after Nabokov)

We made love around tea-time
in the living-room
as though upon a stage
to the accompaniment
of small talk
both of us soberly clothed –
me wearing my best suit
and a polka-dot tie,
she a smart black dress
closed at the throat.
Undergarments were discreetly
parted
rather than being removed,
and with no break in
the chit-chat
and any visible hurry banished
the work was brought to
a tremulous end
in a twisted half-sitting
position on
an uncomfortable little
couch.
A look of dazed ecstasy
idiotised her features
for several seconds
as she sustained her
flippant banter
about work, shoes, star signs,
on the telephone
to a friend.

Blue Hotel

Shadows place themselves

The night rises to swallow us.
An insect fizzes
like a watch being wound.

The trembling hemispheres
of wine in our glasses
slowly tilt and spill...

Called from some remote floor,
the lift arrives.
Doors slide open, suck shut again.

The brightly lit cage
glides downwards
like a diving bell

through the bottomless
ocean
of the hotel.

The Unfaithful Wife
(after Lorca)

To think that I brought her
with me to the river
thinking she was an innocent girl!

It was the night of Santiago
and almost by compunction...
The nightlights were extinguished,
the crickets lit their slow fuse
and at one of the last corners
within earshot of the river
she allowed me to touch her breasts,
which responded, prinking
like branches of hyacinth.
The starch of her petticoat
crackled with static as
my fingers scratched at her thighs.
Past the cypresses and pines
and the limes that afforded us shelter
we could hear the dogs bark
under the horizon...
I removed my tie.
She took off her dress.
I slid off my belt and revolver.
She took off her corset.
I removed my trousers with
a clatter of keys and change.
No carnation had such delicate skin,
aromatic, almost enamelled.
Her muscles flexed like fish
surprised by water first too cold,
then too hot.
That night I gave free rein to
my passion, desire rising from me
like steam from a sweating horse.
As one man to another I would not
wish to repeat what she said
but arrested in the light of sudden
understanding, I felt ridiculed, cheated,
soiled by the sand and her kisses.

I took her from the river and
conducted myself with proper honour.
I felt no love for her then, though
sometime later I did give her
a large sewing box made of coarse straw.

Book at Bedtime

Consider the conjecture
of Schopenhauer
that declares the world
an activity of the mind.

If by accident a moment were to occur
when everyone was asleep,
the world would disappear.

As I read,
the woman gazes at the narrator
and past him at
the amazed reader
over the curve of her naked hip.

The Art of Film
(for William Friedkin)

Japanese, calligraphic.

The city fills with snow
as if picking up static.
A shadow city, a city in negative.

In Monet's Giverney
a leaf falls soundlessly.
Its unreal double flutters up
from the water's depth
to touch it.

And you point out how it's only
when you step
back that the painting resolves
from an original nothingness
into water, trees, light –

the never precisely duplicated
swirl of leaves
twisting in half-circles.

The film over, the screen flashes white.

Meeting Billy

On the way to Paris, lightning struck the *Paramount* jet.
A livid white filament crackled along the aisle.
'That's why I'm late,' Billy explains at the hotel.
Then straightaway he's telling me how he loves the book,
how he thinks it's a masterpiece, how he wants to make
a movie of it and wants me to write the script, that
he's discussed with Placido Domingo the possibility of
an opera, and before I know it, I'm in Bel Air
having travelled first class from LHR to LAX on
a seat with ten possible settings, and champagne on tap.

A cake is delivered with 'Birthday Happy' piped in icing.
Billy blames the syntax on a Mexican confectioner.
He takes me to see Andrew Davis conduct Holst's *The Planets*
and another piece – experimental, dissonant, Stravinskian,
by a young British composer – at the end of which Billy leaps
to his feet to applaud. Loyally I rise to join him.
We leave early, go to the bar. Billy tosses back a whisky
and some peanuts, and works his gums with a toothpick.
He gives the waiter a big tip and says, 'This is for the boys.'

Back at the house, we sit in the den and he's poring over my
first draft. He says, because I'm British, he won't be too salty.
'It's a process,' he tells me, and warns against reviews
and the danger of too much revision. Mahler,
for instance, got terrible reviews, and Bonnard was ejected
from the Louvre for touching up his paintings once they
were on the wall. He's interrupted by a phone call.
'There's a word for that, Mark,' he barks down the line.
'You'll find it in Webster's Concise Dictionary. It's *bullshit*!'
And he slams down the phone. 'Where were we?' he says.

It's the time of the Iraq war. A five star general discloses
the date of the invasion so it won't clash with the opening
of Billy's film. 'It's all about oil,' says the Israeli Secret Service
agent who comes to inspect the house before the Foreign
Minister's visit. 'No,' jokes Billy. 'It's about hummous.'
They need to check the private study where he
keeps his Oscar. Normally no one is allowed inside.
'All right,' he says. 'But I'll have to kill you afterwards.'

Seeing the HOLLYWOOD sign from the Lot, I think of the suicides –
failed actors mostly – dropping from the colossal Os.
And I remember Roger O. Thornhill in *North by Northwest*, who,
asked what his middle initial stands for, says, 'Nothing.'

The dark here happens fast, flattening everything into shadow.
The sky is black, a bowl that empties suddenly.
It's as if the sun just drops off a shelf. The plane
rises into a sky so big you can see the earth is curved.

I wait for lightning to hit, as it did the *Paramount* jet,
but the only lights are those dimmed in the cabin, the only
sound that of the engines merging with the background
hum of the universe.
                        A second passes, then another,
and eventually days and nights and months flow round me.

Birthdays come and go. The war rages on. The planets keep
on spinning. The script lies on my laptop – polished, operatic
and – there's a word for it in the dictionary – unproduced.

Night of the Tightrope Walkers

A curtainless room
on Princes' Avenue,
a flashing Belisha beacon,
the green of the Lloyds Bank sign –
we're in a sleeping bag,
the zip cold against our skin,
and in the silence
at first you resist
but then you let me slide,
your garments to one side.
     Oh, baby.

      *

Through the high wires
from across three seas
via an orbiting satellite
amid oceanic space
across rivers and hills
to the sound of your voice
roughened by sleep
after a second's delay
     – I love you.

      *

Everything is for you –
my waking, the rain,
the sunlight through the window
my poems, these small flowers...

Now I nurse the wound
that heals so slowly
it longs to be re-opened.

No one can hurt me more.

might be thought of as being upside down; it rotates in the opposite direction to all the other planets.

BRENDAN McWILLIAMS, 'Weather Eye', *The Irish Times*

The first time I follow her, she enters a hotel.

Sunstruck, she pulls a hand through her hair, which glitters brilliantly. The glass panels of the revolving door reflect split-second glimpses. Animated, laughing, she sweeps through the lobby, walks as if against a light wind, an absent look on her face. And – is it the space she takes up or the space around her? – an electricity seems generated by her passing, by the sheer vividness of this woman.

I feel my vision tighten. My eyes take her in, an image stored. Black polka-dot neckerchief. Ice-blue eyes. Cheeks high in tone as though fresh from a bath.

Coolly she sails towards the elevator and the trembling bellboy. And then, as the doors suck shut, she is gone.

I can still smell her perfume, trailed like a ribbon behind her, still hear the tick of her heels. No longer solid among us, she hovers – a rumour in the stirred-up lobby, a ghost in a photograph.

Lights burn and voices murmur. Music makes angles in the
air. A ceiling fan whirrs. A black-shirted waiter invites cus-

she stands.

I make my way over, intent on restoring some kind of
balance. I ask her why she's looking at me.

'I like you.'

'You don't know me.'

'We can work on that,' she says.

Amid the riot and clamour, she has the coolness of a flower
shop. Her face is bright and open. There's a blue tint on her
eyelids, a dusting like pollen. The sweetness of her perfume
cuts the sour smell of the bar.

'Here,' she says. 'You'll be needing this.'

'What?'

'My telephone number.'

I run down the street on my way home, weightless,
buoyant. I run until my legs tire, until a stitch afflicts my
side and my lungs begin to burn.

And it occurs to me suddenly that, if all the top crypto-
graphers in the world were asked to decode the mystery of
a woman, to unlock her secret, to discover some invisible
key, after exhaustive investigations this is the answer they'd
come up with: a telephone number freely bestowed.

She drives, while I change gears. We go to the cinema to see *Chungking Express*. She munches her way through a whole tub of popcorn.

'Aren't you worried about all that salt?'

'I can always cry it out,' she says.

At the end, I sit reverentially through the credits. She's restless and ready to leave.

On the way home we both sing *California Dreamin'* over and over again. We narrowly avoid a collision with a big Mercedes going very fast. She leans out the window at what seems a dangerous angle, shouts at the driver of the other car.

I tell her how, for a moment, my heart was in my mouth.

She's not familiar with the expression, asks me to explain it. She says it sounds like something a vampire might say.

My heart, I think. Her mouth.

Half a dozen birds take flight as I open the shutters. Their wings make a *wap wap* sound like a flat tyre. I lean my head

A vivid red strip. As a girl, she tells me, she put on lipstick and practised kissing against her arm, against the mirror, pressing her lips so hard that her teeth would click against the glass.

I'm surprised by her voice this early in the morning. It seems grainier, huskier, more lovely. More foreign.

'Don't fall in love with me,' she says.

'You mean, I have a choice?'

I can see my face in the mirror opposite. My eyes have this faraway look. It's as if I've just glimpsed a vanished paradise.

And maybe I have.

The pipes sing. The taps sparkle. Steam issues like a blessing from the long white mouth of the tub.

'If I'd known, I would have brought a book,' I say when she enters the bathroom.

'What book?'

'*War and Peace.*'

She tuts. '*Anna Karenina* is much better.'

I watch as she twists her hair into a bun, pins it in the mirror. She takes a small bottle from a toilet bag, drops its contents into the bath. A sweet smell lifts to fill the air. Then she steps in, one foot testing the water, the other following. She sits there opposite, her legs astride mine, her arms stretched along the sides of the bath.

The water swings for a moment, rises. She sinks down until the bubbles touch her nose. Suds slop over her breasts. And when she sits up again, skin glistening, the water spills from her body like torn silk.

I think of Tolstoy's women as the glossy knobs of her shoulders are exposed above the water. Her knees form small islands. Her throat grows rosy from the heat. Drops form, elongate, slip from the verdigrised edge of the tap.

I run my finger along the scribble of a blue vein on her ankle, then feel the toughness of her heel, the tautness of her calf, the hollow at the back of her knee. The muscles twitch in her long clean limbs. Her eyes close slowly.

Come to think of it, I wouldn't have done much reading after all.

A hole in the water opens to swallow me.

I swim one complete length underwater. There are bubbles

play on the ceiling — pure energy captured on film. The smell of chlorine mixes with the light, all splintery and squeezed between my lashes.

There is something in me which is always in the pool. And when, hours later, a little dribble of water seeps warmly from my ear, the experience is delicious.

I put my little finger into my ear, wiggle it.

Every time I close my eyes, I see her face. So I close my eyes a lot.

I talk to myself and pretend that she's listening. I write things down so that I won't forget to tell her. I think of funny things to make her laugh.

The bed seems empty and lifeless without her. The silence presses in. The room seems full of things I don't know, that are unknowable. Through the window, the small white hole of the moon pulls everything into it. Dead light.

The secret rhythm of her number comes to me. The repeated bleeps spread outwards like the rings of the city. After nine rings, she picks up.

She's just had a shower, and she's sitting now on her bed, talking to me.

I think of her with lovely fluffed-up hair, her cheeks and throat rosy, her body warm inside her gown.

She says, 'There's no one else there with you?'

'I want you to know that I've been good.'

'Do you miss me?'

Some giant magnet moves unseen beneath the earth, dragging me towards her. And when the line goes dead finally and her voice grows silent, I think of the heat she generates next to me, the hope and wonder she gives off.

I feel her absence like a stone.

I notice a dent in the lampshade, the bubbles in a pane of glass, the pitted surface of a brick beyond the window, a

Where are you?

Two knifelike points of light – car headlights – slice the room. Ghosts swarm, flicker palely. Something inside me swerves.

I feel like an insect trapped inside a bath – the sheer, slippery sides unclimbable, the water beginning to pour.

I remain in the darkened kitchen alone. There are layers and layers of silence. Arms locked round my knees, head bowed, I sit disconsolate, rocking, until you come home.

A fat tomato-red smudge fills the sky above Gatwick. One thing about pollution, it produces better sunsets: all that burnt dust and scattered sunlight. In the distance, a jet penetrates band after band of subtly graduated colour.

I picture you looking down through the scratched window at the river running across the city like a crack across a mirror, at the runway touched with sun.

And I think of you, giddy perhaps after some wine, un-clicking your seatbelt, pulling your coat from the overhead locker, and the music – Vivaldi probably – leaking from the walls of the cabin like the air from the nozzles, now turned off.

A chain of hands reunites you with your luggage. Two little fasteners jiggle where they meet in the middle of your zipped case.

Above us in the car park: a cross of blinking stars.

Another near-miss over Heathrow.

I enter the key card in the door to my room. A green

the blinds, leaving a crimp in one of them.

The night stretches dark and empty, the wind murmurs
thinly. A car shifts gears on the road outside. In pulling the
covers up over me, I pull the silence of the night tight shut
like a purse.

The vulgarity of supermarkets. But now at midnight I enjoy this one.

Music, light and trebly, drizzles from the ceiling as if someone has set the sprinklers off. If it had a flavour, this music, it would be mint. And it mixes with the deep hum of the fridges to create a sensation that I'm floating along with my trolley.

The aisles are a lesson in perspective. Olive paste, basil pesto, chutneys, poppyseeds and cheeses. Rye flakes, muscatel raisins, hazelnuts, chopped apricots and dates. One of the wheels on the trolley keeps going wonky.

The woman in front of me at the checkout swings a dinky designer bag from a single finger. Automatic doors don't open fast enough for her. People exist only to get in her way.

She puts just three items on the conveyor belt: a packet of AA batteries, a bottle of sun lotion and some sanitary towels. A still life. In her hand bag, I glimpse a micro-umbrella, a sexy phone and bottle of water.

What mysteries lurk beneath?

I pack my purchases into thin plastic sacks, whose handles turn instantly to wires in my fists. The doors swing open on the untinted wintry air.

There's a high-pitched squawk as the car alarm clicks off. The lights at the car's four corners wink at me as though knowing something I don't.

The streets are inky, rinsed. I open a window. Raindrops touch my face, trickle slippingly down the windscreen.

painful, more exquisite. Maybe that's what art is, I consider: making moments of melancholy seem beautiful suddenly. The singer hits an impossibly high note: thrilling, hysterical. Listening, I think I detect the hum of suffering behind it all.

The sound of the stereo conceals the tiny sound of the ticking that is the indicator. Unawares, I leave the off-side rear light winking. It's at least a minute before I realise and flick it off.

I take a carton of eggs.

You watch me separate the yolks from their whites, see them slither elastically from palm to palm.

I puncture the yolks with a fork. The mucilaginous liquid slips into a cup containing distilled water. I add white wine vinegar, and stir the eggs with pigments ground to powder and mixed with water to form a paste. Egg tempera.

'You can touch it if you like,' I say.

'It's dry.'

'Yes.'

'That was quick.'

'I told you.' Your fingers reach out and feel the canvas, its toughness, the veins of paint there, the colours: mulberry, umber, dun.

Afterwards, you sniff your fingers. They smell of rotten eggs.

She is vividly present in these sessions: a plait unravelling suddenly; a half-hidden twist of hair; the nap of fabric in a

her left foot: exquisite.

'Why me?' she asks, abruptly.

'What?'

'Why not a proper model?'

I squeeze paint onto a palette from a crumpled tube. The skylight window is open a touch. Quick inky clouds with bits of glitter flit across the glass. The noise of a jet almost drowns me out.

'Because you're beautiful.'

'Stop it.'

'What's it like to wake up in the morning and see how beautiful you are?'

'Everyone in the city looks like me.'

'I live in this city. No one looks like you.'

It seems for a second as though her flesh is dissolving, her inner space rising to the surface. She folds her arms, shyly supporting her breasts, denting them. It's as if she feels undone suddenly, dismantled, as if in the tensely spun mystery of her existence she doesn't belong to herself anymore.

I inhale the nameless scent her skin gives off. The whiff of something coarse and flowery fills the room.

Her clothes, draped carelessly over a chair, slip to the floor like melted wax.

The hills are tan with purply stains, as if someone has spilt wine on them. And there's the sudsy upwards push of the sea, its ceaseless rhythms and tireless voice that, heard over and over, become hypnotically a kind of song.

Gulls flap like bits of torn paper. The sun touches the headland like a thought. The sand is ribbed beneath our feet, and our shadows wobble there. The water is chill, glittery, achingly cold. Little waves slap upwards over my tummy.

I stretch out star-like on my back. My eyes close. The skin behind my lids turns red.

We float, holding hands, allowing the breeze to twist us in gentle circles. Then, salty, exalted, we swim out further. I kiss her, pushing back her hair. Her limbs are slick, her body elongated like a Modigliani in the water. We swim again, buoyed not just by the water, but by something light inside us – an invisible gas: happiness. We laugh, and for a few minutes don't care about anything or anyone else. And suddenly everything is very funny as I send a long thin fountain of foam upwards from my mouth.

The clay was warm the day God made her.
From the pallid breasts to the light honey of the shoulders,

same plane of remoteness as the stars.

He senses a splendour in her. She glows for him. In her presence, he feels close to the hidden quickness of things.

He tries to catch his feelings for this woman, to arrest the seethe he feels within him. His paintings offer her up in different tints, from various angles, a series of fractional views. Put together, he feels they constitute a kind of truth. Week by week the studies mount up. Sketch after sketch, painting after painting – he does not know how many – thickening into a secret body of work. Fields of colour, vivid brilliancies – citrus, pink, vermilion – a luminosity fierce and tender. And there she is, at the centre of them, bright as a light bulb, with that electric texture to her skin, a fine-grained pallor that seems almost unearthly.

With his energies perpetually refreshed, he feels something beyond him pushing him on, directing each brush-stroke, dictating every dab. He experiences it as a kind of sunburst, a heat released within him. The canvases seem radiant spaces, warm and changing as the tones of human skin.

There have been other brief glimmers, instants of vision, moments of ecstasy, privileged glimpses of something brighter breaking through. But he's never managed to sustain them before. And now, in wishing to affirm his love, to sing its existence, in the blind wish and impulse to say yes, he's wary of the potential for any falling off. He watches for it like the first drops of rain, like a dog bothered by its shadow.

She fills a bowl with baked beans for the children, punches out the time and presses POWER on the microwave – three blips, a high beep, then the rising hum of its cooking.

The digits count down to zero. Three loud bleeps signal that the beans are ready.

Standing by the kitchen window, she draws shapes in the condensation. The glass is cold, squeaks a little. She presses the finger to her cheek and the feeling is delicious. Everything around her in this instant seems especially vivid: the feathery branches of the conifers elastic in the wind, the colours of the sky melting from pink to mauve, and the tight weave of the carpet beneath her feet, the blue seeming to tremble and leap out.

She slides open the French windows, admitting a cold blast of air. She breathes in deeply, filling her lungs. Then a sensation overtakes her: it's as if she's falling. The pull of negative spaces. The tops of the trees grow blurry. The sky darkens visibly. The carpet seems to rise to meet her. She tugs the window shut again.

In the renewed silence, she feels the warmth creep back into the room, sees the trees retreat to a safe distance, the tide in the carpet ebb.

In hoicking it off you seem to pour yourself upwards. Your
head snags in the tunnel of your jumper. The nubbly wool

ing in a kind of infinitesimal seesaw, a sensation of fulness
ebbing. Soon we are both drowsy and becalmed, your face
nestled against my shoulder. And through this sleepiness, I
hear you whisper. I can barely make out what you say, but
know that you're repeating the sweetest things. It settles in
my ears as a kind of hum.

The bleaching sweep of headlights tilts the angles of the
room. Your touch stays with me. And where your fingers
linger, it feels as if a wound has been opened then stitched
with silk.

I fall into a long nothingness. A steep sorrow.

Sleep.

I open the door to the bedroom and see my son, his face white in the darkness. He grows quiet as I approach. I lift him out, offer him a drink from a plastic cup. He insists with an infant's greediness on drinking down to the bottom. Stupefied with milk, he points back absently at the cot. He's getting heavy. Having lost that babyish weightlessness, he has taken on a definite heft.

His sleepy peaceful face hovers like a little moon. His cheeks are hectic, his brow feverish with dreams, his hands damp and clammy. Braced as though for a fall, he lies with his hands spread above his head.

I kiss his flushed face, stroke his carroty curls, and say goodnight. I hear him smack his lips. And I watch for a second as he scratches his head in drowsy puzzlement. I listen for the familiar rhythm of his breathing, watch for the up and down movement of his chest. The memory of his heaviness is still in my arms.

He's asleep before I reach the door.

In my one recurring dream, I'm with my father. We're in a department store. He's holding my hand. I'm five-years-old.

words won't come out right.

Moments unroll. Then beyond the circle of faces, I see him, a few yards away. He's looking at me, arms folded, smiling.

Afterwards he repeats three things:

'I love you.'

And: 'I won't always be here.'

And: 'You have to be strong.'

Driving, she feels she's in a cocoon, a protective bubble. She notices how, as if by magic, droplets of rain tremble upwards on the windscreen, forced back by the wind and speed of the car. She sings along to Barbara Lewis, 'Baby, I'm Yours...' Around her, other cars skim lightly, as if self-propelled, gliding like sprung toys on a track.

She decides – even though it's raining – to go into the car wash. She collects the tokens and mounts the stand. The machine whirrs into action. Its bars advance implacably with a sense of menace, then stop. Sustained sprays of water follow. Squirts of detergent blur her vision. A rush of suds pours over the glass. The windscreen resembles a membrane that refuses to break. Fluffy giant rollers swarm against the sides of the car, flailing against the windows, drumming across the roof.

She feels closed-in, assaulted by the world's hard corners.

Abruptly the whole car is in shadow. She regrets it now, and wants to get out. She shrinks into her seat and closes her eyes. 'I must be crazy,' she says. 'What am I doing?' Her only defence, she realises, is a kind of amorous delirium.

Some force has acted upon her, unhinged her, made her do things that are reckless and incredible. Those people who claim that love is a social construct have obviously never experienced it for themselves.

Everything grows quiet now except for a slow dripping.

She raises herself in the seat, switches on the ignition and starts forward slowly. The wipers clear the windscreen. Beads of water drip from the treads of the tyres. The bonnet gleams as though painted anew. She turns on the headlights. Shadows wheel and tilt in front of her. The beams are full of sparkling rain.

The cassette re-engages. She feels something brim within her. The songs of strong women fill the car.

I see her everywhere – obliquely in a shop window, coming up the subway stairs, through the windscreen of a passing

The generosity of spirit extends outwards, so that I open doors for people, perform a thousand small courtesies, allow cars to feed into the lane in front of me, readily surrender my place in a queue. The feeling of largesse fills me like a gas.

It's like those photographs of war-torn cities where, amid the ruins, one building stands upright, glittering in the sun; or like a melody sustained above the chaos by a single hovering chord.

The one clean note: happiness.

This cold late afternoon in March, I see you ahead of me outside the Hayward Gallery. I watch for a second and recognise the gesture as you lift your mittened fingers to push the hair away from your eyes.

Afterwards we walk hand-in-hand over the Hungerford Bridge. To our right, a train slides along the rails like a strip of film being fed through the city. To our left, the traffic flows unceasingly in strings of red and white lights.

It begins to rain. Your umbrella carves for both of us a bell-shaped space. And in the cold we seem surrounded by odours. A host of different scents lifts upwards composed of your raincoat, the tang of wet hair, and the hard sweetness of my aftershave.

A red bus swishes past massively like a light ship. The warm wind from its wake breaks against us with its whiff of diesel oil. 'Come back with me,' I say.

Your face takes on the blue tint of the umbrella. 'Now?'

I watch as, in another treasurable gesture, you shift your weight from left to right and tilt your head the other way.

A muggy night, heavy with the sweat of vegetation and people. There will be a storm.

lamp next to your head makes a low continuous buzzing. The noise hovers with the energy of a conscience.

What is it you want anyway? A man cast entire from your fantasies? A man so perfect it's as if he's been distilled from some precipitate of your will?

As you sit there attempting to read, a strange thing happens. Perhaps you nod off for a moment. Either that or you must choose an especially soft part of the bed because, beneath your weight, the mattress seems to give and you feel yourself falling.

It's an instant of terror, like those moments when you're tumbling in a dream. Or when you press the pedal and see beneath your feet the train's blurred hurtle, hear the sudden vortical roar.

I always know when it's about to happen. The atmosphere grows heavy. The atoms around me tighten and vibrate. I hear a remote high-voltage hum. Without warning, everything disintegrates: walls fall away, people melt into dead space, and the fear contracts to a hard seed inside me. I have difficulty breathing. It's as if the air is slowly sucked out of the room.

I hear this voice. I recognise it. My father's. I'm not imagining it. It emerges through a surrounding hiss as though from a radio station, the wavelength slightly awry. His voice floats, feathery, the broadcast of a ghost.

I can make out just a few words. Something about hoping that it's not too late, and that I must forgive him. And for a moment he seems very close. The darkness presses fold upon fold.

Then I hear him tell me I'm alone in the world.

Glancing across, he sees the skin above his wife's nightie both over and through his glasses.

that each pore, each individual cell, each molecule comes into focus revealing ever more layers beneath.

He makes a show of setting down his book, removing his glasses and switching off the bedside light. He snuggles down into the covers. Then he stretches his arm across her tummy. 'I'm sorry.'

She ignores him, continues to read.

'I'm sorry,' he tries again. And then, 'I love you.'

He begins to caress her stomach, the tops of her legs – nothing she could object to. After a minute, his hands widen in slow circles to touch the base of her breasts, her tidy triangle of hair. His movements are so gentle, he knows it would seem odd for her to protest. He diddles her nipples, and she makes it plain that she's not interested. She's reading, she says. But he's not to be discouraged. He returns to those slow circles. He persists, knowing that there's a kind of routine by now between the two of them in their lovemaking, a slow inevitability. She resists his touch, and he senses her reluctance. But he hears her gulp. She snaps a page over.

'No,' she says, slapping his hand.

He carries on, more gently but just as insistently.

'I said, no. I mean it.'

He ignores her and continues. He's reclaiming her, reestablishing his authority. He feels her legs twitch. It is some time now since she has turned a page. Something animal gathers itself and overtakes them both.

He makes love to her, though she hardly participates, averting her mouth from his kisses as if he has bad breath. Still, she trembles violently to a climax, and he enjoys watching her eyes slide into that familiar whiteness like the snow.

'Why didn't you ring me yesterday?' she says, when next she speaks to him on the phone. She tortured herself the previous evening waiting for his call.

'I wasn't sure you wanted me to.'

'You're right. I'm not sure I did.'

'Meaning?'

'Maybe you'd better not call again.'

A silence follows, a stone dropped into the void. She stands in the hall, plucking chrysanthemum petals, rolling them into thin tubes.

'You're joking.'

'Of course,' she says. 'Are you?'

He says nothing.

She dares, 'I love you.' She wants the words to be light, but they sound, to her own ears, heavy and solemn. She had imagined them both, by some miracle of synchronicity, uttering these words without warning, together in the same breath. A simultaneous avowal.

There's a pause in which she hears a whistle in the crack of his breathing, her words flung out on an impulse into the dark.

'I mean it,' she says. Contained in her voice is a warning.

He says, 'So do I.'

Adultery has a colour, red. And a taste, dark and sweet.

It is a heavy thing, this loving, she reflects. The feeling

She starts to unload the dishwasher, busying herself lifting each plate and glass. She puts them back in the cupboard exactly where they should go. Steam rises from the machine. The glasses are hot still and scald her hands.

She refills the machine, and fishes a tablet from the packet. She hates that powdery smell, the chalky feel of it.

Later, still tipsy from the wine and unable to sleep, she hears the dishwasher begin its new cycle, feels it kick so hard it hurts.

He sees himself on a video monitor in a shop window, distorted, foreshortened, black and white. He stares back at his reflected image. For a moment, he hardly recognises himself: bleached cheeks, an elongated torso, dark shadows gathered under his eyes. He moves out, then back into shot.

Already, he thinks, it will be possible to plot his progress and chart his whereabouts on a series of video security cameras mounted on gantries around the capital. Already his ghostly negative is stored as part of the ceaseless thrilling hiss of information which constitutes the city.

He wanders on until he reaches the river. Across the water the flags of other European nation states snap lumpily in the wind. The flagpoles jiggle, and the sound carries faintly like the agitation of tiny bells. He gazes at the water, its crumply reflections.

Fucking England, he thinks. This soggy crowded island, with its consumption of newspapers and tea, its football hooligans and slowly eroding coastline. Fucking England with its olde worlde coffee shops, its graceless cuisine, its net curtains, and strawberries and cream. Fucking England with its guest houses, its high streets all the same, its love of pets, and its men who swim with their glasses on in the pools of foreign hotels. Fucking England.

A nation of cloud worshippers.

He watches the water flow in volatile whorls, in unstable loops and spirals.

The idea of drowning suddenly enters his head. The twisted grace of his body tugged under by the tide, bubbles unravelling from his mouth, the water darkening as he plunges deeper, the light reduced to a pinprick, his soul just squeezing through.

When the trap door opens, what strikes her first is the smell:
a strong odour of turps and varnish, a hint of toxicity. Rain

the lustrous fruit of breasts. Body parts. And different colours,
reminding her of those luminous wonky squares you get in
Kandinsky and Klee. There is something musical in the scales
of colour, fine distinctions of shade: honey, oak, caramel,
tan, apricot, plum, and that sudden bit of orange that in a
Monet turns out to be the sun.

At first she thinks they are different women. But slowly
the perception grows upon her that the model is the same.
Floating luminous nudes. Nudes falling into radiance, ex-
posed on white sheets. Nudes seen from the front, or dorsally
– in private and in silence everywhere she looks.

There's a granular texture to them, too, she notices – noth-
ing deodorised or lacquered, nothing glossy. The paint is
applied in gobs, with squirts of pigment, slashes of colour.
There are patches, too, where the paint is deliberately nicked,
thinned-out. Amid the manipulations of light and shade,
there are spurts of blue where veins run shallowly, inflections
of red on the face and throat, dashes of russet and grape
about the trunk. The nipples, she sees, have the brown colour
that only women who have had children possess – not the
pre-parturition pink of her own.

In most of them the model seems to be sleeping, supine
or prone, lolling like an odalisque on a sofa or bed.

Then it strikes her. A presence hovers over them, as if in
a fogged mirror. She senses a female smell inside the room.

She shakes her head, sweeps her hair back with her hand.
She can't believe it. It's her own face she's looking at.

'Shit!' she says, out loud.

We wake to the whiteness of sheets and curdled sunlight. The snow sparkles with a brilliance that makes us wince. A marvellous transparency inhabits everything: the clarity of blue March days. The world is dazzling, glassy, the trees precisely outlined.

The snow has come late this year, then come in a rush. But the smell of pines and the blue of the sky, like an up-turned bowl, make it good.

The instructor tells me to loosen up, to be more supple, to bend my knees and swivel more, leaning my weight into each turn.

'Don't resist the fall,' he says again. 'Accept it.'

I love the burning in the lungs as you hurtle down, the snow's crispness smoking, the distant magic of the hills, the whole hiss and shush of it. It's so quiet, the smallest noise becomes audible – the flap of a bird's wings, a hank of snow slipping from a tree. A whisper is amplified into a shout. The crack of a branch twangs in the air, the lift machinery clanks, and the sound of snow crunched underfoot is loud as a radish in your mouth.

At night we feel sealed in here, with the snow gently falling. And then when it clears, the stars seem round and fat like fruit. The sky slides back like a planetarium to reveal the moon.

The gritting machines are out on the roads. Salt crackles drily beneath passing tyres, is driven by the wind into eddying

to the perpendicular. The night is p
cold. Bunching a coat sleeve over his hand, he tries to scrape away the glaze. Little filigrees adhere to his fingers, sticky as sugar to the touch. From his wallet he slides a credit card. He chips away with the card's edge until the ice falls away in larger chunks.

Opposite, a neighbour drives a shovel in a series of gravelly slurps.

In the rear-view mirror, his green eyes shine like leaked anti-freeze. His chin is tricked out with the beginnings of a beard. His fingers come together with a rasp around the jaw like the sound a hand makes as it's dragged across a microphone.

He starts the car, plays the accelerator, hears the engine climb the scale before relaxing into an even purr. White clouds pour from the exhaust and seem to congeal in the freezing air.

Inch by inch, the condensation and traces of ice evaporate from the glass.

The traffic is impossibly sclerotic. It takes an hour to get across the bricky suburbs. The light is so dim still, the street-lamps remain on. The streaky surfaces and wet prisms of the capital reel in and out the mirror. A parallel text of offices and shops.

On the radio, some American Santa says that British Santas aren't doing their job properly. They don't even know the correct number of elves, he says, or the names of the rein-deer. The speaker is a recent graduate of the Santa Claus Foundation in Greenland and claims that British Father Christmases are dull and grumpy. He says they should wear classier outfits, cultivate a certain seasonal magic and have the ability to visualise the North Pole.

All around him, the snow hatches a kind of privacy. Big wet flakes swarm. One snags in his lashes and trembles there.

A pink streetlamp fibrillates, blinks. His corneas sting in the wind. Car horns mingle with the faint strains of muzak trickling from the stores. A drill starts not far away. The radio on a dispatch rider's motorbike squawks.

Then abruptly cutting through the traffic, with the hiss of air-brakes and a clamorous siren, an ambulance tears down the street. The letters on the front are written backwards.

The snowflakes seem ionised, as though tugged by some hidden force.

For a wild instant he imagines her in that ambulance, semi-conscious, repeating as if in a stupor, half-audibly, his name.

The world shrinks to a vivid point of pain.

Feeling kissy in the back of a taxi, we're driven through the city – a series of blurry chromes in the rain.

the door. The lights change and the windscreen is _____
with colour.

I pick off one long hair from my coat. It clings to my fingers. And with a show of nonchalance that startles even myself, I do not once look back.

Brandishing a thick rubber-handled torch, I unlock the door and step out into the starless darkness and the snow.

I feel curiously light, afflicted with a kind of dizziness. The cold and the wind press through me. The darkness seems an extension of myself.

The flashlight's beam skids against the walls of the house, the fence, and jiggles its zero across the grass.

I point the torch up into the sky.

It reflects nothing back, just blackness. Blackness and silence. And whatever lies beyond.